Frank M. Wanderer

THE REVOLUTION OF CONSCIOUSNESS

De-conditioning the Programmed Mind

Author: Frank M. Wanderer
(margif61@gmail.com)

Editor: Ervin K. Kery
(kery.org@gmail.com)

Proofreading: Melissa Jennewein
(onenomadwoman@gmail.com)

(c) 2015 Frank M. Wanderer, Ervin K. Kery

www.consciousnessbooks.cf
www.frankmwanderer.com

ISBN-13: 978-1512333916
ISBN-10: 1512333913
BISAC: Self-Help / Spiritual

*The revolution of the Consciousness is
taking place Now,
in the present moment.
There are no strategies, no great leaders in
this revolution,
only heroes who understand
the evolutionary progress of the
Consciousness
and are open to allow the processes to take
place in themselves*

CONTENTS

The Revolution of Consciousness

If we take a look at the events of our world, we will easily realize that we live in revolutionary times. The revolution of our days is, however, entirely different from any other revolutions in human history. This revolution is not launched in order to rearrange the domain of forms and shapes, so as to replace old and outdated forms and shapes with new, dynamic and vivid ones. This revolution is able to take humanity beyond forms and shapes. The revolution of our time is the revolution of the Consciousness.

Consciousness, which has been sound asleep under the spell of identification with the forms and shapes for thousands of years, is slowly waking up in our days. There is an increasingly powerful alarming impulse, and the number of people sensitive to the wake up call is getting bigger and bigger.

The effects of this impulse, waking us up from our dream of identification with the forms and shapes is felt by everybody, sometimes even several times a day. But many of us are unaware of what we actually experience; all we feel is that successes achievable in the world are less and less attractive for us. We recognize that behind earthly successes and failures there has to be something deeper, something more profound in our life.

We see it day by day that an increasing number of young people question the appropriateness of the goals offered by social and religious education. They shake off the hands trying to lead them along the right track, and as a consequence, they are exposed to the experience of emptiness and despair.

Society offers a "solution" for the problem, in the form of the products of the entertainment and pharmaceutical industries and the manufacturers and service providers of excise goods and services. Today, these are prospering and extremely lucrative industries. They offer "help" to young people in suppressing fear and in treating other superficial symptoms.

There is only one gateway leading out of this situation: and that is the present moment. We are only able to shift the center of gravity of our life from the peripheries to the center. What does it mean?

The edge is the present state of Consciousness, in which the overwhelming majority of people live. That is the state of identifying with the mind, that of the dormant Consciousness, which dreams and tells our personal history.

That is the state of perfect identification with thoughts, emotions and desires, where we seek the goals of our life only in the world of forms and shapes, whether they are crude material forms (the world experienced with our sensory organs) or fine material forms (thoughts, emotions). The motor of our existence on the edge is the ambition to become something or somebody and to be in control all the time.

The center-point, the Awakened Consciousness, and the world of internal silence are beyond the mind. It does not refer to the internal silence forced upon oneself by various techniques called meditation (in this case, in fact concentration), but the indescribable, *but experiential, alive and living internal emptiness.* In there, there is no effort, no desire and ambition, and we give up the last bastion of wanting to be in control. This is the state of perfect abandonment and submission, submitting ourselves to the Present Moment, to the Now.

The revolution of the Consciousness is therefore taking place Now, in the present moment. There are no strategies, no great leaders in this revolution, only heroes who understand the evolutionary progress of the Consciousness and are open to allow the processes to take place in themselves.

The Biggest Illusion of the World

We live here on Earth, together with billions of fellow human beings. That we live is an irrefutable empirical fact. Similarly, the fact that other people live on Earth, too, is also an empirical fact. We do not merely live, however, but we are also personalities. We are personalities who are similar to each other in various respects, and largely different from each other in other respects. That we are personalities, different from each other is also an empirical fact for us. Out of these two experiences, however, only one is true, the other is deception. Only one is a fact, the other is an illusion, and the biggest illusion in the world at that.

The Beginnings of the Illusion

Let us take a closer look and examine which of the two experiences is true and which is a mere illusion.

Our life in this world begins when we are born. It is obvious that we are alive, but we are not yet a personality. At that time only the simplicity and greatness of the present, the existence is known to us.

The society, and its culture, is what shapes us into personalities while we grow up. We become a personality when our Ego is born. This is an inevitable step in the evolution of the Consciousness, so there is nothing wrong with that. The Ego is born, the separate little Self, as a focus of the Consciousness. That little Self obtains experience about itself and the world. In the natural course of evolution and as a result of the experience gathered, the Ego withdraws to give way to the process as a result of which Consciousness awakens to its own existence through a human form.

The progress of this evolutionary process can, however, be impeded by an illusion: the illusion that the individual is becoming somebody, a personality. We begin to become somebody, a personality, when we start to identify with the Ego, with that separate little Self. Under that illusion we believe that the Ego is a reality, and we are identical with the Ego, and the development of the separate little Self is in fact the foundation of our personal development. Nowadays it is virtually impossible to avoid that kind of illusion, since mankind has lived in it for thousands of years. The deception has become independent, and the illusion of the Ego is now a reality for the entire mankind, including, naturally, us.

The Nature of the Illusion

Our identification with the Ego makes us therefore somebody, a personality. On the other hand, our identification with the Ego will be the root of all our problems and misery. Since around us everybody considers the Ego as the most important centre of their life, we are also brought up by our parents to have a powerful Ego, a centre point in our life, by the time we reach adulthood. It is necessary because our society–and its culture–favors and worships the individuals with a powerful Ego.

Our parents and teachers bring us up in the spirit of the permanent endeavors to become somebody, to become a strong personality, to become somebody different from what are now (to become bigger, more important and better than other people). That is why we always watch other people, we compare and measure ourselves to them. All that time, we also try to adjust our actions and deeds to the expectations and opinions of others. We keep dealing with the past and the future, and we never have sufficient time to stop and notice the immense illusion behind our life.

The End of the Illusion

An illusion may only survive if it is continually fanned and nourished. If we take a look around through innocent eyes (that is, through eyes free of any kind of opinion) we will soon realize how every society nourishes and fans, through its various institutions, the illusion of the separate little Self, the Ego. How they nourish the illusion of "somebody-ness" in us and in everybody else. All that may take place because every society, every culture is based upon individuals, and if those individuals disappear, they wake up from their "somebody-ness," the former *modus operandi* of that society collapses.

That is why Eckhart Tolle is perfectly right when he asserts that the world can only change from inside. The internal change means that we wake up from our "somebody-ness" and we begin to understand what our mission is in the evolutionary progress of the Consciousness.

We must therefore wake up from the illusion of our "somebody-ness" in order to concentrate our attention on reality. That reality is nothing but the innermost empirical fact in our life, that is, the fact that we live, and we constitute a vibrating Consciousness, full of life. That is the reality that has been shrouded from us by the illusion, the mistake that we concentrated all our efforts on sustaining our "somebody-ness."

If we stop nourishing that illusion, it will vanish after a while. In order to severe the power line of the illusion, we must learn how to notice the vividness and beauty of the present moment. Once we are able to accept the present moment, we are able to accept ourselves and we are able to enjoy the simplicity, tranquility and peace of existence. The Ego and the experience of "somebody-ness" then disappear, and we remain nothing but pure, vibrating energy, Life itself.

In the Web of the Spider

Everybody has their own personal history. Our parents began to weave our personal history; first they told us who we were, they relayed the rules of living in a community, together with other people within a specific society. Then the little Ego was born in us, and we started to listen to the voice of the Ego that began to tell us our personal history. The inner voice told us a story about who we were and which way our life was heading. We found the story so convincing that it never even occurred to us to question its truth. But is this story really true, or is this just the Ego, babbling away and leading us into the cobweb of thoughts hopelessly?

The Anatomy of our Personal History

Every waking moment of our life fits a personal history with our own Self in its focus. Our life can only be interpreted within the framework of that history. The reason for that is that we identify with the voice of the Ego, the narrator of our own story, so closely that our personal history becomes the foundation of our entire life.

A closer look at that personal history will, however, reveal that our internal story consists of a fabric of experiences and thoughts. Thoughts that explain our experiences, thoughts that we believe and with which we identified, thoughts that will thus provide the foundations of our self-determination.

Our personal history keeps us under its spell, in a hypnotic state in which all our attention is devoted to the inner voice and story it tells. In this way we give up our alertness, the world passes by us, because we only concentrate on the elements of reality that appear to confirm our personal history. We therefore lose our grip on the deeper dimensions of life. The deeper dimensions are present in our life, but we lose contact with them because of our lack of alertness.

Beyond the Personal History

The question may arise in us whether we are really identical with our own personal history, or perhaps we are more than that? Everybody has some vague suspicion that our personal history does not reflect reality, we are in fact at a deeper level than that.

When everything is apparently all right in our personal history, we achieve our goals, we are happy, and the vague suspicion vanishes entirely in us, and our identification with our personal history becomes more powerful. There are, however, moments in our life when nothing appears to succeed, so we are unhappy and we suffer. The suspicion then reinforces in us, and we tend to believe that we are more than the cluster of thoughts that constitute our personal history. We realize that we are more than mere thoughts.

As long as we insist on our personal history, and on the storyteller, the deeper dimensions of our existence remain inaccessible for us. Not because these deeper dimensions are not present in our life, but because weaving the web of our personal history engages all our attention.

Waking up from our Personal History

If we become aware and conscious of our own personal history that we are telling ourselves, we have a chance to wake up from the hypnotic spell of our personal history.

In order to become aware and conscious of our personal history, we must ask ourself the question, "*Who is it, talking in my head, who is this inner voice, telling me my own personal history?"* The only possible honest answer to that question is, that *"I have no idea!"* Any other answer is rooted in the personal history, and as such, it is to be rejected.

The honest answer may easily be a shock for us, completely uprooting our life the way we lived it previously. The more closely we identified with our personal history, the bigger our astonishment may be. We no longer believe in what we have firmly regarded as our own personal history. This experience may, however, lead us to the point of questioning the truth of what we believed to be true in connection with ourselves.

This is the first sign that we begin to wake up from the hypnotic effect of our personal history. Now our attention is no longer fully engaged by our personal history, the storyteller telling us the story, and our identification with the story. We may then become sensitive to the deeper dimensions of our life.

We are the Entirety of Existence

The gateway leading us to the deeper dimensions of Life is Alertness, which appears as a result of the release of our attention from the hypnotic state of listening to our personal story. The new Alertness enables us to learn about ourselves without identifying with our thoughts and emotions.

What we first experience in this new, alert state beyond our thoughts and emotions is the completeness of existence. In that state all fragmentation disappears from our life, we recognize the inner spaciousness of our existence, our inner happiness and tranquility. We feel at home in our own skin, and we realize that our alert consciousness is free from all kinds of thoughts and emotions.

We then may decide whether we wish to continue to listen to our personal story, or we move further on, towards the quiet foundations of our existence.

The Secret of the Inner Voice

"Tell me, what do you think about me, what is your opinion about me?" we have asked other people this question a number of times. We were, however, not interested in the opinion of just anyone; we only wanted to know the opinion of others who have been close to us: our family members, teachers and friends. All through our life, we have collected these opinions, we have been staring at the mirror. In the view of what we see in the mirror, we make efforts to find an answer to the most important question of our life: Who am I?

With what we have gathered from the opinions received from others, we forged an image of ourselves, who we are and what our mission in life is. We have gradually identified with the image, we believed that the image is really us; we have pinned it up on the wall of our room, and proudly show it to any coming our way: look, that is me.

On the other hand, the image in the mirror has also caused us a lot of worry, since there is always a doubt in us: does that image really meet the expectations of others, do we appear good, decent, religious enough in the eyes of others?

As a consequence, we spend our whole life polishing and improving the image in order to make it look better and better for others. We tend to believe that the best strategy in this process is copying, imitating others. This is a strategy that we use from our babyhood onward, that is how we learn our native language, and that is how we acquire the elements of our culture. Later, when we are older, we continue copying others, since if we follow the ways of those who lead a decent and good life, we cannot be wrong.

Another characteristic feature of our image in the mirror is that it is contradictory by nature. We receive almost as many opinions as we have friends and acquaintances. Some may consider us as clever, whereas others do not find that the most important feature of ours. It generates a permanent state of uncertainty in connection with the image, that is, in connection with ourselves.

This uncertainty in connection with ourselves shall serve as a basis for our desire to convince other people that the image in the mirror is true, and we really are the way other people see us. If our identification with the image in the mirror -generated from the opinions of others- is strong, it keeps us in a virtually hypnotic state, and we live our whole life under the spell of that image.

It is, however, a gross mistake to believe that we see our real face in the mirror of opinions. No opinion is able to reflect our real self, our real, inner existence, and it is impossible to project our real, inner self onto any mirror.

If we intend to really know ourself, we have to be able to turn away from the mirror of opinions. We should no longer deal with what others think about us; instead, we need to concentrate on who we really are. For example, the real issue for us is not whether others see us as happy, but whether we are really happy.

The mirror of opinions will not release its victim very easily, though. It has been so deeply incorporated into our personality that it is in fact a real part of our personality. Whenever we attempt to turn away from the mirror of opinions, an inner voice, the voice of our consciousness will, speaks to us: "what are my parents going to say? What would my wife think about it?" This inner voice is very often quite effective, and we are again under the hypnotic spell of the image in the mirror.

For breaking out of the spell, we need to understand that the only way of knowing ourselves is through direct experience, our own experience, and not through the opinion of others. We are only able to receive direct experience if we are alert. So as to be alert, we need to focus our attention to the Here and Now.

If, in an alert state of mind, we submerge into the present moment, we shall experience a miracle. The mirror of opinions blurs, and our wholesome Self, the pleasure of Existence shall be revealed.

The Obstacle to Enlightenment

In our present, individual state of consciousness we identify with the thoughts and emotions that appear in our mind, so we believe that we are a separate, illusionary person, an Ego. The truth is that we are the embodiment of Life, we are born into this world as a result of a miracle, and later we are lost amidst the multitude of teachings and dogmas. After identifying with our beliefs and convictions we forget who we really are, who the person born into the world in order to experience existence and get acquainted with all the teachings is. A sign of awakening is when we realize that the state when we identify with our Ego is of very low order, very poor, and there are more significant mysteries behind our existence. Only the consciousness of the present moment is able to terminate the illusory self-interpretation and elevate the person's consciousness to a higher, more spiritual level.

What is an Ego?

The Ego is the central figure of our personal history, based upon the past and looking into the future. The components of the Ego are thoughts, emotions, memories (with which the person identifies as "my story"), fixed unconscious roles and collective identifications (nationality, religion, etc.). Most people completely identify with these components of the Ego, and for them no self "outside" of this exists.

The Ego is shaped by the past, determining its structure and contents. The structure of the Ego is an unconscious factor, which forces the individual to reinforce his/her identity by joining an external object. The content of the Ego will then be the thing with which the individual has identified him/herself with (my house, my car, my child, my intelligence, my opinion, etc.). The contents of the Ego (with which the individual identifies) are shaped by the environment and upbringing of the person, that is, the culture in which the person becomes an adult.

The identification of the Ego with things (object, the person's own body, way of thinking) creates the link of the individual to various things. The Ego (and thus the spiritually unconscious person) experiences his/her existence through the possession of various objects. The satisfaction provided by the sense of possession is, however, short, so the individual usually carries on the pursuit for new objects. There is a powerful motivation behind this activity of the individual, a psychological demand to obtain more, the unconscious sense of "not yet enough," and this feeling surfaces in a want for more. This want is a more powerful driving force for the Ego than the desire to possess. The uneasy feelings, recklessness, boredom, stress and dissatisfaction are all largely the products of the dissatisfied longing for more.

The thoughts such as "it's mine," "I want it," "I need it," "it is not enough," belong to the structure of the Ego. The content of the Ego changes with time; it is replaced with new contents. No content is, however, able to lastingly satisfy the Ego as long as the structure of the Ego remains in its place. The individual keeps looking for something different, something that promises a greater satisfaction, making the sense of self of the individual more complete.

This structure determines the various functions of the Ego. In Eckhart Tolle's opinion the most important of the functions are the following:

- The Ego strives to protect, sustain and expand itself,
- The Ego functions in survival mode.

One of the most important strategies of the Ego to sustain and reinforce itself is the experience of "I am right." This is the identification of an idea, position, evaluation. Nothing gives the Ego more power than experiencing that "I am right."

One of the favorite self-reinforcing strategies of the Ego is complaining. Complaining implies the sense that "I am right." When another Ego refuses to accept that "I am right," it is an offense to the complaining Ego, which in turn, further reinforces its self-awareness.

The statement that the Ego functions in a survival mode means that it continually struggles to remain "psychologically alive," so it regards other Egos as rivals or even enemies. It is the desire of the Ego to be right, and thus overcome the other, ensuring its own superiority.

The Ego is a Small Part of the Personality

If we wish to understand how the Ego works, we must not disregard the fact that Ego is only a small part of our personality. Ego is a part of the personality, and its content comes from our sensory perceptions and memories (our life history and knowledge and experience gathered throughout our life). Ego is the thinking, feeling and sensing part. The part of our Ego we show the external world is termed by Carl G. Jung as *Persona*, the acting personality. That part of the Ego is foregrounded when we are in the company of other people. That is, in fact, the collection of our masks.

A large part of the personality is constituted by the unconscious Ego, termed by Freud as the instinctive Ego. That is where our most basic instincts (eating, sexuality etc.) are found, and also the part of the personality described by Carl Gustav Jung as the *Shadow*. The "Shadow" is shaped and developed by society, almost simultaneously with our role playing personality. Children, when they wish to meet their parents'–and through them, society's–expectations, begin to develop these masks. These masks are like what the environment shapes them to be. Rejecting certain stimuli offered by the environment triggers the disapproval of our teachers, so the intention to reject stimuli is suppressed. That is how our "shadow-personality" develops. It does exist within our personality, but our education relegates it into our subconscious.

Freud believes that the third important component of our personality is the *Superego.* It comprises the social values that the culture in which we grow up finds important. In the course of a long and complicated process these values are incorporated into our personality and manifests as the ideal self (the person we would like to be). These values become integral, inner parts of the personality, and surface as opinion and conviction.

The findings of psychological research suggest that more than 90% of the functions of the personality are unconscious. Large parts of the Instinct-Ego, the Persona and the Superego are unconscious. The functions of the Ego are also largely unconscious.

The Ego is responsible for the integrity of the personality, for our inner well-being. This is no small task for the Ego, as it is constantly bombarded by unconscious expectations from the Instinct Ego and the Shadow, attempting to influence its behavior. It generates anguish in the Ego (that is, in ourselves), manifested as discomfort (we do not feel all right). The Ego wishes to escape from the anguish, so it also uses subconscious mechanisms. Such a mechanism is, for instance, projection. The Ego projects the unacceptable desires and features coming from the Shadow and Instinct Ego onto others (e. g. I am not aggressive, you are aggressive). These subconscious, protective and anguish eliminating projections are the foundations of several of the mind games to be discussed later.

Beyond the Ego

The Ego is not bad, it is simply unconscious. Ego is the deepest dream of the Consciousness. If an individual is able to notice and observe the functions of the Ego, he or she will be able to transcend it. In that case, the individual who has been looking for a more complete perception of the self will recognize that it has always been there, but the functions of the Ego—identification with objects and thoughts—have pushed it into the background. One of the ways of transcending the Ego is not reacting wholeheartedly to the ever-changing kaleidoscope of thoughts and emotions, but concentrating on the alert consciousness in the background instead.

In most people, the term "consciousness" identifies with that socially conditioned Ego. For a number of people this identification is so powerful that they are unaware that their life is governed by a socially conditioned mind.

Those who are able to go beyond that identification with the mind recognize this state of being socially conditioned, and are also able to leave the social conditioning behind. Such a person will not identify with the mind but, increasingly, with the Consciousness (the Witnessing Presence). The Presence shall, therefore, control the mind to an increasing extent and will be manifested through the tranquilized mind.

The Power of the Conditioned Mind

The society and culture in which you have grown up programmed those fixed patterns of the mind into you, and your identity who you are and what your job is in this world, is based upon those patterns. These systematic patterns of thoughts, programmed into you by your parents and teachers are deeply embedded into your mind and subconscious by the psychological mechanisms of identification, and they automatically surface every now and then.

Whether you like it or not, these thoughts come and go, and your mind is in constant motion. These patterns strive to be self-sustaining, and they generate the work of the mind. The result is the cobweb of thoughts with which you identify and that is how you live your life.

In-Depth Programming of the Mind

The fixed patterns of your mind are individual, since they reflect the expectations of the particular environment in which you have been brought up. The expectations usually influence you unconsciously, almost like automatic deep programs of the mind.

As these in-depth conditionings have become a part of your mind in the course of your upbringing, a particular situation or person immediately activates them. You automatically put on the mask appropriate for the particular situation, tailored to the expectations of the situation or person.

You must recognize that it is not the expectations that constitute the problem. The expectations are natural parts of the world of forms and shapes. You are not able to exist without expectations in the society you live in at present, just like you would not be able to exist without your body.

The compelling force of the expectations is fed by your identification with them and the fact that you stick to your personal identity and the masks and expectations that come with it even after you have woken up.

Through their compelling force, the fixed mental patterns are powerfully influential. Their power is in accordance with the degree of your identification with them. The more you believe in your own thoughts, the more powerful they will be over you, and they will easily obscure your Sight and, by reducing your Alertness, they will drag you back to your world of dreams.

Closing the Gates

In order to make your awakening irrevocable, you first need to recognize your fixed mental patterns! Once you have seen and recognized them, you are able to shut the doors leading back to your dream world, just left behind, one by one.

It does not mean that you need to shut the doors yourself. The fixed operational methods of the mind cannot be defeated by the works of the mind itself, that is, by effort, practice or your willpower.

When a fixed mental pattern appears, all you need to do is watch how it works, what expectation activates it. But you do not need to fight it, you do not need to make any effort to neutralize it.

There is only one remedy against them, and that is Sight, nourished by the deeper dimensions of Alertness, and the Sight will bring recognition to you. The power of Sight is that it reduces your identification with your mind, and places you back into your original state of existence, that is, Oneness.

When you see and recognize how your fixed mental patterns work, the energy supply they receive gradually dries up, since the energy that formerly supplied these patterns now supply the emergence of the deeper dimensions of Alertness in you. In this way, conditioned mental patterns gradually lose their power and they vanish. As a result, the work of the mind that might have appeared chaotic to you before becoming increasingly transparent.

In this way, Consciousness and Presence will increasingly dominate your mind, and they will be manifested in longer and longer periods of silence. That is how the mind regains its original mission, and it will become a means by which Consciousness is able to express itself in the world of forms and shapes.

6 Steps and 3 Awakenings on the Spiritual Path

You are invited on a special journey, in the course of which our inner light–which is our sympathy with others–shines up in us, purified and free of all concepts formerly attached to it. It is, however, important to make sure that the pure inner light should not shine for ourselves only, but for everyone who is seeking it. The light of our sympathy should reach the most remote corners of existence, in order to show others the way leading out of suffering. That is how we are able to become credible helpers for the spiritual seekers. This journey takes us through six steps to three awakenings, each one more profound than the previous one. In the following we wish to discuss these steps in more detail.

1. Step. The first awakening: the world of permanent change

Our whole life is a rush. We chase our desires and unfulfilled dreams. We are attracted by money, power, prestige, a wholesome, happy life. All of this lies there hidden behind the powerful iron gate that is towering in front of us.

Spurred by our ambitions, we pursue various goals all through our lives. We aspire for something all the time, we always want to achieve something. This restless rush is instigated by our fear that we are still not what we want to be. We are never satisfied, we always want something else, we would like to be better, more beautiful, richer than we are at present.

That is how we pursue our goals until death, when we realize how meaningless the whole thing has been. But why are these goals meaningless, we begin to protest immediately. The protest is caused by the vary nature of the forms and shapes, as in their world every form and shape is subject to permanent change, birth and death. Whatever we attract to us, we are going to lose it, as everybody departs from this world empty-handed, all those who pursue their goals, live in the spell of past and future.

Our first awakening therefore shows us the real nature of the world, its constant change.

2. Step. The spiritual seeking

We, however, wish to find the security of permanence in our life. We would like to find what is beyond the world of constant change. In order to do so, we become spiritual seekers.

As a first step of spiritual seeking we start to look for enlightenment, Self-recognition in the world of shapes and forms (that is, outside ourselves) in the hope of thus reaching the state of permanent happiness. We intend to find a dogma, a great Master, an elevating spiritual experience that expands our Consciousness. If it is not found here on Earth, we will be looking for it in the other world, in the heaven of a religion.

We use the mind as a means of spiritual search. It is through the mind that the Ego intends to understand what is beyond mind and forms. The mind in this way prepares the mental image of enlightenment, seeking, happiness etc.

The mental images are born through the comprehensive process of the mind. For comprehension, we also require information, so we shall gather bits of information like a busy ant. From books on religion and spirituality, lectures heard and conversations attended, we are attempting to screen information, ideas, opinions and experiences necessary for them. The same takes place with spiritual experience. We assume that if we gather a sufficient amount of experience, as a result we will reach a certain point, and we will increase our spirituality.

These mental images motivate us to make efforts at implementing the mental images at the level of daily life, to make these images the cornerstones of our life. Achieving spiritual objectives, however, affords only momentary satisfaction for us, so after achieving one specific goal, relentlessness returns, urging us to start working for new objectives. The mind produces new mental images, and seeking starts all over again.

3. Step. The second awakening: the stop

We then go on seeking, until we eventually become tired of the process, and finally recognize its true nature. That is when we arrive at our second awakening.

We stop and abandon spiritual seeking. We recognize that all the objectives we have so far been looking for outside ourselves, are only found within ourselves.

We will stop when we recognize the activities of the mind and refuse to follow it any longer. We realize that with the help of the mind we will not be able to surpass the mind. We will experience that stopping is the inactive moment of the mind, the silence between thoughts. In that silence, we will experience the Consciousness without forms, and recognize that we are in fact the Presence without thoughts. We then leave behind the spiritual seeker, with all the accumulated knowledge and lofty spiritual experience.

4.Step. The inner journey

We then embark on an inner journey that will take us beyond the Mind. Once we have started our journey, we leave the world behind and abandon everything that has hampered us in our progress. We give up unimportant things in order to be able to concentrate our attention exclusively on the important ones. That is possible by means of a major mental clean-up.

When we begin doing that clean-up in earnest, we will soon face the vast multitude of our thoughts, opinions, ideas and the emotions attached to all these.

After a period of time, we realize that we need to abandon all the unimportant things and trivialities, since these things will be found false in the light of our inner journey. Then we find ourselves all alone, and realize, that we still have not finished. We are still to shed the shadow that we believed to be ourself.

5. Step. The third awakening: Coming home

The third awaking is the awakening of the Conscience to its own existence through the form and shape that we formerly identified with ourselves. After the great clean up nothing remains but the empty space.

But if we examine that space closer, we find that it is full of Consciousness, which is the inner peace, quiet and tranquility. We then realize that we are at home. Whatever now happens in that internal space, we must experience that. We must experience whatever life has to offer, there and then in that specific moment. The next moment does not need to bear the burden of the experience of the previous moment.

Now the question arises whether it is really the end of our journey? The emptiness is now perfect, but we still need to make the last step in order to become credible spiritual helpers.

6. Step. Comeback

That step will take us to the point where our entire journey began. We return to the world of daily life. We, however, return in a state different from the one in which we departed, since we have undergone considerable changes during our journey. The Mind, the Ego and, together with it, selfishness vanished from ourselves. The emptiness, pulsating with life, and the Consciousness, awakened to its own existence, continue to stay with us. The most beautiful flower of this state of existence is our sympathy with others.

In this way the world will be entirely different for us. We no longer feel an urge to run away from it, and we do not submerge in the swamp of identifying with the world. We are now free from all that, and the world is now a new adventure for us. We abandon ourselves into the streams of Life, and we merge with the Universe. In the meanwhile, we help others in awakening and we share the joy of existence and sympathy with everyone we encounter during our journey.

How the Higher Levels of Consciousness may Appear in our Life?

When we are asked what we find is the most important thing in our life, most of us would be able to answer the question. We would, naturally, come up with different answers, but that is not the point; the point is that we are able to answer. But as long as we are able to answer, we remain detached from the higher levels of Consciousness. How is that possible?

The Nature of Higher Consciousness

If we wish to find out how that is possible, we must first examine the nature of higher Consciousness. A number of people have experienced those higher levels, and there are thousands of reports about that state of Consciousness.

Still, if we penetrate deep into that experience, we find that no higher levels of Consciousness exist, only Consciousness itself. That Consciousness has only two states that we are able to experience: one identified with various forms and shapes, and one that is free of forms and shapes.

The Consciousness Identified with the Forms and Shapes

What does this identification mean? It means that we identify with a form (e. g. our name) that originally did not belong to us (we are all born without a name), but through identification this specific form has become a part of our existence.

When the Consciousness identifies with a form, the Ego appears. The Ego always means some sort of an identification, self-determination (I am a man, I am a father, I am an Englishman, I am Christian etc.) The Ego therefore rests upon our identification with things that are important for our ego. If I am able to answer the question, "What is important for me?" I am in the state of identification with the forms and shapes.

This state of Consciousness is always restrictive and exclusive. Identification is always preceded by a process of selection: this thing–this form–is important for me, whereas that one is not. We usually choose the forms and shapes that we find beautiful, good and valuable, since these are expected to make us beautiful, good and valuable people. Selection always comes hand in hand with anxiety and fear that we may lose what is important for us and, together with those things, we may lose ourselves.

The process of identification does not stop just because we have become spiritual helpers. But now different things are becoming important for us, for instance the extended state of Consciousness or the experience of the astral projection. At that state of Consciousness, we identify with these experiences, these are the factors that are important for us, they provide the identity of our spiritual Ego. Nothing has really changed, apart from the forms and shapes we identify with.

The Consciousness Free from Forms and Shapes

There are moments in everybody's life when our identification with the forms and shapes loosens a little bit for a short while, and in that instant we may experience an entirely different state of Consciousness.

When our identification with a form ceases, a new space is generated between us and the form and we are able to see and recognize that we are not identical with that form. With the dissolution of the identification, the Ego also disappears. When we are in that state of Consciousness and we are asked what we find important in life, we are simply unable to answer the question, as everything that we formerly regarded as important vanished together with the Ego. Still, we sense that we are alive, and we did not disappear with the Ego.

What we then experience may perhaps be best termed as Being. There is only the pure existence, we are eyewitnesses, contemplating the dance of forms and shapes around us. We do not identify with anything, we are a Consciousness free of the obligation to make choices. We are free and independent of the forms and shapes and of the necessity of choosing from them. All our suffering and problems have vanished, and we are surrounded by peace and tranquility.

Awakening from the Stupor of Identifications

On most occasions, one is only able to experience that state of Consciousness free of identifications for very brief periods. This is, however, one of the most wonderful and certainly one of the most important experiences in our life. It wakes us up, in fact shakes us out of the stupor of identifications.

Once we have had that experience, our alertness will increase, and we will pay more and more attention to the present moment. When we are alert and shift the center of our existence into the "here and now," our identification with the forms and shapes will further loosen. Such moments may therefore appear more and more frequently in our life. As we are bound to the forms and shapes to a lesser and lesser degree, the periods and intensity of these experiences increases. In the end it will remain the only reality for us.

The Currents of Love

Intimacy is one of the most elementary human needs. Its shortage deteriorates, its wealth nourishes human soul. One of the most beautiful expression of intimacy is when two people embrace each other. This wonderful human gesture is a store of great secrets. What are the secrets of embrace? Embrace has a smaller and a greater secret.

The Small Secret of Embrace

The small secret of embrace is that it has a wide range of positive physiological and psychological effects. For instance, it increases trust and confidence, it reduces anxiety, fear, and pain, and alleviates the aftermath of stress.

An embrace means closeness and warmth in human relations, it is the most intimate expression of love. An embrace reinforces connections, it affords a sense of safety and improves the intensity of two people's sense of belonging together. An embrace is a form of communication, with it we may express things that we are not able to put into words.

An embrace provides us with an exceptionally intensive sense of belonging to another person. It is not possible to generate the same emotion in any other way. An embrace tranquilizes the soul and, for a few moments, is able to make us forget the things and problems around us.

An Embrace as a Gateway

In an embrace, our whole body is permeated by currents of energy, giving us a fine, pleasant feeling. This energy is love. In the embrace, in this current of love, a gateway opens up. Through the gate, some of our original state of existence shines through. This is the great secret of embrace.

Our original state of existence is a state in which Consciousness is not identified with forms and shapes. This state of the Consciousness is Life itself, the state of Oneness, and empty space filled up completely with the vibrating energy of love that encompasses everything else.

In our present state of Consciousness we identify with the forms and shapes, and thus we are separated from the Oneness. In that state, most of us have forgotten our original state of existence. Nowadays, the majority of people consider the Ego, that small, detached Self, as reality. That is the consequence of our identification with the world of forms and shapes.

An embrace is, however, able to dissolve our identification with the forms and shapes, we open up for the other person, we become receptive, and the Ego disappears. The stream of our thoughts stop, and only the present moment exists for us. Then, at that moment of alertness, we receive something from the immense, universal current of love coming to us through the gate that has opened up for us. Consciousness may wake up to its own existence, it may escape from the spell of identification with the forms and shapes.

That is why it is useful to make use of the gateway opened up by an embrace as frequently as possible in our daily life. A hug to you all!

The Secret of the Constructive Energy

Most of the time we are indifferent, and we are afraid to react to the small vibrations of life. We hold up that indifference as a protective shield in front of us and that is how we live the weekdays of our life. It is true that the shield of "Who cares" protects us from a lot of nuisance in life, but a high price is exerted for that protection. Indifference makes us insensitive, and insensitive in turn prevents us from abandoning ourselves into the constructive energy of Life. What is that constructive energy and what is its secret?

Nowadays, most of us lack the main components of that constructive energy: creativity, spontaneity, vitality and drive. In the lack of these strains we live for ourselves as isolated Egos in a world which is generally characterized by stress, aggression, unhappiness and a lack of love. This is because the most of us hide under the cloak of indifference.

In such a world, fewer and fewer of us feel all right, we would like to change it somehow. If we do want to change it, we should not expect the change from others, we must initiate the change ourselves. We might as well start the change by shedding the cloak of indifference. How are we going to be able to accomplish that?

The deepest source of indifference in us is the fact that we live as separate and isolated Egos and, most of the time, our attention is engaged by telling our personal history. The fibers of the fabric of our personal history are constituted by our opinions and experiences. We devote almost all the energy of our life to make that fabric more and more individual, beautiful and colorful. We remain indifferent to all the things and persons who do not help us in pursuit of that goal. In the case of most people, the process is unconscious, people do not recognize it, as they tend to powerfully identify with their own personal histories.

In the face of what has been described above, it is clear that once we are able to stop telling our own personal history, and we are able to wake up from the spell, the cloak of indifference may fall from our shoulders. Upon that awakening we immediately find ourselves in Life, in the current of pure, constructive energy. We will be filled with vividness, coupled with creativity, spontaneity and drive. In this way happiness and love are incorporated into our life.

We must therefore wake up from the hypnosis of our identification with our personal life story. Quite a lot of us, however, make the awakening a part of our personal story, and convert the awakening itself into an objective to be achieved in the future. Awakening is, however, not attainable as a part of our own personal history.

Awakening means that we have to be alert. We are only able to be alert here and now, in the present moment, and not some time in the future. So, if we wish to wake up, we have to be present in every act of ours, we must be present with deep concentration and full devotion. In this way, any act we perform, no matter how insignificant it might appear, will be a constructive action.

Making efforts to be alert should be a guideline in our life. Let us make no difference between small and great things, all our actions should be permeated by alert concentration.

Once we have become alert to the present moment, indifference will simply disappear from our life, giving way to constructive energy. That is how we will become full of life, full of creative energy, and we enter the world of unconditional love, and our actions will be the source of radiation of that love.

An Effective Remedy for the Overburdened Mind

Our Mind is one of the most sophisticated, most complicated instruments in the world. In this modern, rushing world, however, the Mind is bombarded with information to the extent that it virtually overflows. On those occasions the amounts of unprocessed information whirl in the Mind so fast that we are sometimes afraid of going mad. All the unprocessed information demands our attention, naturally, every single idea may appear to be very important for us. Our body reacts to the rushing stream of our thoughts, and sometime we fall ill because of the stress caused by our overburdened Mind. Is there anything that we may do to alleviate the burden of our Mind, is there a medicine to treat the problem?

Naturally, the remedy exists, and its name is meditation. A good night's sleep in itself has long been insufficient for our Mind to rest. At night our body sleeps, but the our Mind continues to rush. The enormous amounts of information absorbed during the day are processed by our Mind at night. It is done with the help of dreaming. Thus, by the time our Mind has finished processing the information, our body is awake again, and a new day, full of stimuli begins. Our Mind therefore does not have its due share of rest, and it is soon overburdened. All this leads to a stressful life, and our body may eventually become ill.

We have to consciously find the time for our Mind to have some relaxation and to have an opportunity to shake out all that useless information. We must therefore find the place for meditation in our daily timetable. During meditation, the Mind rearranges itself, it is refreshed and revitalized and rejuvenated.

Meditation is a subtle, barely perceptible stream, in which you will experience a radical shift of the center of gravity. The manifestation, limited in time and space, thick and heavy, that you have formerly regarded as yourself, changes into a weightless but ubiquitous point without limits and dimensions. The massive creature, bound to the earth that used to be you, is now free from its bonds and begins to soar. That is what happens when you occupy the timeless time and space-less space of the

Contemplating Presence, which is eternally in the Here and Now.

We must apply this medicine, this treatment called meditation every day in order to preserve the balance of our Mind, and to save it from becoming overburdened again. How should we use the medicine?

Every day, we must withdraw from the world for half an hour or an hour, we need to be completely alone. We need to consciously and completely empty our Mind, so that no thought, no emotion, no memory remains in it. All we need to do is be alert, that is the essence of meditation. If we perform that every day, our Mind ceases to be overburdened, it is refreshed, recharged with energy and regains its balance. Free space emerges in our Mind, giving way to the free roaming of our Consciousness.

Experience the Deeper Dimensions of Mindfulness

Recognizing yourself as Consciousness is independent of all the activities of the mind. This recognition will only come if you have had some experience of the deeper dimensions of Mindfulness.

When you experience the deeper dimensions of Mindfulness you stop and at the same time you exit from your personal history and give up searching. It means that you divert your attention from the world of forms and shapes, and you no longer wish to find yourself in the world of forms.

Stopping is the consequence of a shift of attention within your Consciousness. Stopping does not mean the stoppage of your mind, as you have assumed previously. Some of the spiritual teachings suggest that stoppage is equal to emptying the mind, usually through various, forced exercises. The mind will, naturally, stop, but you will not need to impose it on yourself by spiritual exercises, as it will be the consequence of the shift of attention in your consciousness.

How does this shift take place? It is not something one is able to force or impose upon them; no effort is capable of achieving that. It is an experience that simply happens to you. That is when you experience something from the deeper dimensions of Mindfulness.

This is not something that may only occur to the chosen few. It has happened to almost every human being, including you, a few times. You were not alert enough, that is why you failed to realize what was happening to you. At the moment when the shift of attention is taking place Mindfulness emerges. A space appears in you, you have the ability of seeing, and you may contemplate what is happening to you as an external observer.

Then, like in a flashlight, you see and recognize the reality of your existence, that is, you are not an illusionary small self, but a Consciousness free of forms. That recognition is not the result of the analytical work of the mind, but of a series of realizations inspired by the inner quiet. These realizations can be best compared to seeing (that is why various spiritual teachings refer to such people as Seers) and it works like a revelation. That is what I call *the power of Sight.*

Though the moments of Sight are rare in the life of a person, they are available to everyone, who is aware of them, alert, and pays attention to them. The level of your Mindfulness is therefore what determines whether the experience is a real turning point in your life, or the Sight is blurred, you fall back to sleep and continue dreaming your personal history.

Sight brings you the experience that stoppage is an inactive moment of the mind, silence between thoughts. In that silence you experience consciousness without forms, and you may recognize that you are in fact a Presence without thoughts.

In the moments of Sight you recognize the activities of mind, and you no longer follow them. You recognize the simple fact that with the help of the mind you are not able to reach beyond the mind.

By experiencing the deeper dimensions of Mindfulness, the capability of Sight, you also recognize that you are fully independent of the mind, you are but a witness of what is happening in and around you. Once you have ceased to identify with your mind, you immediately experience that fact. That is why you should detach yourself from the mind, and stay in the position of the eyewitness. That is the state of spatial consciousness, in which the light of Consciousness, Presence shines out bright.

The Secret of Silence

The world around us is too noisy, we are constantly surrounded by the murmur of the civilized world. We have almost completely forgotten today, how living a silent life in this noisy world could be. What secret could the silence have?

The mystery of silence becomes interesting for us when we become spiritual seekers. From that time on, we start looking for the essence of life, we wish to find an answer to the question:

"Who am I, and what is my mission on this Earth?"

We first look for the answer in the external world. We try to find an idea, an ideology and we identify with it in order to look for the answers to the questions that preoccupy us and cause that tormenting sense of want that spurred us to embark on a quest for answers.

After a lot of futile efforts we realize that no idea, ideology, teacher or master is able to provide us a satisfactory answer to those questions. We then turn inward, and start looking for the answers in ourselves.

Turning inwards requires quiet and tranquility from us, so silence becomes important for us from that time on. We find a quiet corner for ourselves where we are able to think and meditate without being disturbed. We leave behind civilization, go to the mountains, nature or the loneliness of a monastery.

Here at first we believe that we have found what we were looking for, because the quiet of nature, or the quiet life of a closed community surrounds us, and the silence we have found gives us satisfaction and happiness. If we are able to tranquilize the noisy world inside our head in this peaceful environment, external silence may be followed by meditation after a while. The forced internal silence and temporary tranquility is the result of the suppression of thinking. *This silence is, however, not our own, it is not a part of our soul.*

It is aptly demonstrated by the fact that when we return to the noisy revolving stage of society, and are surrounded by the vivid world of a big city, our hard-acquired tranquility is gone immediately, our cherished silence disappears as if it had never existed. If we are lucky, and the external world remains silent around us, only the silence of our meditation is lost every time when the mind starts working, and thoughts and emotions flood our brain.

All this shows that there is something wrong with us, we were completely mistaken when we believed that the magic power of silence will set us free of ourselves. The problem is that were looking in the wrong direction when we thought that silence is something outside ourselves, something that we are able to achieve by suppressing the work of the mind.

Silence is one of the qualities of the Miracle, that is our own Self, the Consciousness. We have therefore never lost it, because we cannot lose what we ourselves are. We need to find our inner Self again by allowing Consciousness to wake up to itself in us.

From that time on the silence will always remain with us, we no longer need to look for it in the external world or force it upon us by suppressing our stream of thoughts. After that, no matter where we are in the world, even at the noisiest railway station, we will never lose our inner silence, our Self.

There is Nobody out there but You

We, who strive to achieve spiritual development, often have the feeling that certain people or situations impede that development. There is a number of things that may hamper us in our progress along our spiritual way. Sometime people find bad karma as the gravest obstacle in their spiritual progress. We were born in the wrong place, under the wrong circumstances; we should deal with those circumstances first, and start our spiritual development only afterwards. Is that really so?

If we want to answer that question, we must examine one of the most effective defensive mechanisms of our Mind, that is, finding a scapegoat. It means that whenever we encounter difficulties in our life, we tend to look for the reason of the problem outside ourselves. We blame the responsibility on external factors or persons which or who may cause our difficulties.

When we believe that our bad karma prevents us from making progress and spiritual development, we are relieved, since we cannot help it, it is not our fault, things just work out that way. We have all the good will but, unfortunately, adverse circumstances interfered and curbed us in implementing our great intentions. We therefore wait for a more favorable occasion, and tend to put ourselves in the position of the victim.

This attitude appears to be logical, but it is not. Whatever may happen to us in life, and whatever difficulty we face, in most cases, comes about as a consequence of our previous actions and choices. No matter what is happening to us in the present moment, that is the outcome of our previous, unconscious actions, we sowed the seed from which our present difficulties sprang up. We are not the victims of circumstances; on the contrary. We create and operate the bad karma we complain about and on which we wish to blame responsibility for our bad luck.

We must change that attitude in order to be able to break out of the vicious circle. Our attitude will only change if we recognize that there is nobody and nothing we are able to place responsibility on, but ourselves. We must therefore give up looking for excuses, and we must shoulder the responsibility for our actions and for our spiritual development. There is nobody but ourselves in the way of our own spiritual progress, we ourselves have blocked the way with our previous attitudes.

The truth is that we are now set free of our bad karma. Freedom means that now, in the present moment, we act consciously and do what the present moment requires us to do. Naturally, in order to be able to do that, we must submit to the present moment, the present circumstances. That conscious surrender means that we do not resist the present moment, we do not attempt to run away from it, but try to bring ourselves into an inner harmony with what we have in the present moment.

Our inner harmony with the specific situation means that we fully accept that situation. So as to accept the situation, it is necessary for us to be alert, we need to be present in that specific situation. Being consciously open, we will recognize and clearly see what the situation demands from us. Whatever we do in that state of complete alertness, will not be the cause of any bad karma, since our action is in accordance with the possibilities and requirements of the situation concerned.

Then, if in lack of alertness, we make the wrong decisions, we must accept responsibility for the consequences. Accepting responsibility in turns means that we accept the circumstances and, become alert to the specific situation, we find the path leading to the right decisions. That is how real intelligence streams into our actions, and that is how the present moment becomes a teacher in our spiritual journey.

The Secret of Enlightenment: Be Yourself!

The ultimate goal of our spiritual quest is enlightenment, that is what we all wish to achieve. But why do we seek enlightenment? Perhaps because at present we feel that we are not yet what we should rightfully be, we are not yet enlightened. What can be the reason we are under that impression? In the first years of our life it never occurred to us that we needed to change, we needed to become somebody else, that we were in need of enlightenment. Then, some time during our life, that urge arose in us. It is imperative that we examine the circumstances and reasons why that emotion appeared in us, since it is that very emotion that prevents us from becoming enlightened.

Enlightenment is not a remote state of Consciousness that we need to achieve some time in the future, but it is the very heart of our nature. Our spiritual quest, however, diverts our attention to that imaginary, future state of Consciousness that we believe to be enlightenment. In this way, the spiritual quest detaches and diverts us from our true nature, enlightenment. We are therefore unable to ever reach enlightenment through the process of spiritual quest.

Enlightenment is, as we can now see, our true, inner nature. But what is in our true, inner nature? Unfortunately, during our spiritual search, most of us have been alienated from it; so much so, that we have even forgotten about it. It is, however, permanently present in our life, but we simply disregard it. Our attention is always engaged by something, something that we need to deal with, so we very rarely take the trouble of looking into ourself. Still, if we were able to concentrate our attention on ourselves, that brief moment of alert Consciousness would be enough for us to recognize that the alert Consciousness, free of emotions and thoughts is our true inner nature. We are now enlightened, we have never been anything else.

The question now arises, where has that enlightenment, that alert consciousness disappeared from our life? As children, playing free of problems, we live in the present moment, in the state of alert Consciousness (so if we wish to meet an enlightened human being, all we need to do is go out to the nearest playground).

Then, carefree playing was replaced by more serious things in our life. From our parents we learned who we are and what our mission in life is. We were told that we are young human beings, still in the process of developing and shaping, and becoming an adult is a hard work.

Carefree playing was gradually replaced by purpose-oriented work in our life. Our teachers and parents therefore taught as how to set up objectives, how to make plans, and we soon learned that future is more important for us than present. We then concentrated our attention from the vividness of the present moment into the image our parents and teachers created in us, into the image we need to become one day. Simultaneously with that process, the impression that we are not what we are supposed to be emerged gradually in our mind.

As children we simply had no choice, we had to accept the process, we had to identify with the new image. We are therefore moving away from our own inner nature, under the hypnotic attraction of a future goal to be achieved later. It is thus understandable that we look upon enlightenment as a goal to be achieved in the future.

Spurred by our ambitions, we pursue various goals all through our lives. Our whole life is a rush. We chase our desires and unfulfilled dreams. We are attracted by money, power, prestige, a wholesome, happy life. We aspire for something all the time, we always want to achieve something. This restless rush is instigated by our fear that we are still not what we want to be. We are never satisfied, we always want something else, we would like to be better, more beautiful, richer than we are at present.

Everybody nurtures an idealized image of what he/she would like to be like. The mind projects this idealized image into the future, and reveals the way leading to it. But this image requires a constant rush, stress, anxiety and worry in our life, as nothing is free, we have to struggle to achieve our goals.

But this is not our own personal tragedy, but that of the entire mankind. Generation after generation is conditioned to that attitude by the preceding generations. It is a vicious circle, and breaking out of it is almost impossible.

During our spiritual journey we must recognize this process, and we must realize that we no longer need to become something new, as we are all in possession of all the qualities that we have been pursuing so far in our dreams.

We must make efforts to be present at every moment of our life. That Presence shall bring alert Consciousness back to our life. In the state of alert Consciousness thoughts will no longer keep our attention in captivity, and we may experience silence. In the alert silence we recognize that it is our real Self, it is our real inner nature. Enlightenment is us, we ourselves.

Learn How to Live in the Flow of Life

On the ordinary days of our life, you work, educate your children, have some fun, build and sustain connections with others, that is, you live an ordinary life. The question is, whether you are mindful during all these things, or you just perform these activities mechanically, automatically.

What is the evidence for me that you are not mindful? First, that *you are not present*. To be present means that you are fully alert, attentive, and conscious in the present moment. Whatever you do, you do that fully consciously, you focus your entire attention on that particular activity. Or, do you feel free to declare that you are present in every moment of your life?

You are careless most of the time, as a large segment of your attention is bound by dealing with events of your thoughts, events of past and plans for future and your own self. Psychological time therefore displaces the moment of the present, or subordinates it to past or future.

You therefore perform the overwhelming majority of your daily activities mechanically. Your attention only becomes more intensive when you meet someone or deal with something who or that you find interesting, or useful in some way. Or the opposite: the person or thing may do harm to you in some way.

If you are mindful, only the Here and Now exist for you. This state of consciousness is characterized by deep silence and tranquility.

You could ask, how could you access this state of consciousness?
I would answer you, that in your life you have already lived through this mind state, more than once.

On the gray veil of ordinary consciousness, there are gaps every now and then, and the bright light of the Consciousness shines through the gaps. The gaps are too small for you to get through, but have a glimpse to the reality behind the wall.

Such moments are rare in the life of a man, but they are still there for all those who pay attention and want to see them. The toys of your daily life, however, occupy all your attention so much that you do not even notice the opportunity that opens up for you, and your attention slips away from the Miracle.

When you submerge in your ordinary consciousness, your attention keeps wandering from past to future. The moments of insight are, however, only available in the Present, only if you leave behind the psychological time, the memories of the past and the expectations of the future all vanish, and you are able to focus your attention to the Miracle that unfolds in front of your eyes in the Present.

It has happened to you that you came under the spell of a moment some time during your life. A beautiful landscape, a sunset, a beautiful piece of art, the rhythm of music enchanted you. It may even happen that you are just lost in the silence of a peaceful moment.

The common feature of these moments is the mind stops working, the reckless stream of thoughts is suspended. Ego disappears, telling personal history stops, and the line of your accustomed identity is broken. Only the spell of the moment, the mysterious shine of the Consciousness remains.

Why is this moment so enchanting, what is its secret? The secret is that when thoughts disappear, so do your problems and conflicts, and you almost forget about all your sufferings. You virtually step out of the psychological time frame, you stop mulling over injuries of the past, and do not build your identity for the future.

You are mindful, only the present moment exists for you. Your soul is permeated by the quiet of the Consciousness and the Joy of the Existence. The world is alive, pulsating around you, and you are amazed to realize, how wonderful it is to be alive. You believe that you are only alive now.

You submit to the moment, sitting in your favorite armchair or lying on the beach, listening to the noises of your environment, enjoying the rest, the sunshine and fresh air. *Both past and future are far away from you, only the present moment matters. As if a heavy curtain would have been drawn away in front of your eyes; now everything is more vivid and brighter around you. You feel that you are alive, and it is good to be alive. The Miracle almost completely fills your soul. Why could it not stay that way forever?*

Unfortunately, these moments do not last long, because the mind starts working again very soon, and begins to control the moment by categorizing it and giving it a name. *"Ah, yes, how beautiful is this sunset"* and the tumbleweed of thinking starts tumbling again:*"It reminds me of last summer, when…"*.

Your alert attention will then turn away from the Miracle, back to the mind, and your ordinary identity is rebuilt in a matter of a few seconds. You return to the psychological time and, embedded into it, you experience your problems and sufferings again. The memory of the moments of spell is just a transient impression, the unconscious feeling that some miraculous thing happened to you, but you unfortunately missed a chance. Indeed, you missed the chance of entering through the gate opening in the magic moment and finding your real Self there.

Can you do something in order not to let this happen anymore? *What is able to put an end to that Vicious Circle?*

You are only able to escape if you are able to proceed beyond the mind, if you terminate your unconscious identification with it, so you are able get out of the vicious circle. In that case you are able to observe the functions of the mind and realize that you are by no means identical with your mind and its functions. You are identical with the pure space, the Consciousness, in which the functions of the mind take place.

If you are able to leave behind all the scenarios of your identity built up by the mind, even that of the Spiritual Seeker, you may experience that this Consciousness is really you. You are the pure space of the Consciousness, the existence, which is your real Self.

Your real Self is beyond every thought, every social program instilled into you. This Miracle cannot be described by thoughts, it is only possible to experience it by direct experience.

But not even the word "to experience" expresses the essence of the process very well, as experiencing is just a thought, too. This experience is the experience of the awakening Consciousness, and words are only able to point at it like fingers, but are unable to express its essence.

The Miracle may perhaps be best described in words in the following way: *You will be united with the Consciousness living in you, and you will recognize the forms and shapes appearing in the space of the Consciousness as part of that Oneness.*

About the Author

Frank M. Wanderer
(Ph.D, Prof. of Psychology, consciousness researcher, writer)

the Consciousness leads sonal history to the pure iousness. There we racle, and all personal significant. Despite this, sent a few pages of my the reader, as every starts with a personal history. That is the only way it may start, there is no alternative; that is the only way leading to the awakening of the Consciousness, the appearance of the Miracle.

Since my early childhood, I have been interested in the Miracle, the mystery of human existence, the *mystery that summoned us from the Nothing, and the mystery we are destined to solve in our life.*

I still remember my beloved mother's astonished face when, after some of my questions, she turned to the others: "Now, look at that, what that kid is asking!"

The questions did not stop in the later years but, as I did not find an appropriate partner from whom I could expect answers, the questions mostly remained within the walls of my room, and I myself attempted to find the answers.

My motivation became even more powerful after the following adventure: I was at the elementary school (12 years old), walking home from school and suddenly I experienced the Miracle, the completeness, the experience of the unity with the Self. At that time, naturally, I was not able to describe it that way, but the sense of unity and happiness was what I experienced.

That experience did not result in my lasting awakening, it faded away after a while, but it left behind a burning wound, a real sense of want. At the same time, it showed me the way, where to look for the answers to my questions.

There was a long way to go to the second awakening. The first awakening made me start dealing with esoterica and find books on the subject.

Leaving the years of childhood behind, in my adulthood I became intensively interested in the human soul, in the work of the human mind.

As a teacher and psychologist I have met a lot of people, and had an opportunity to study the "normal" operation of human ego, and also its functions that are considered as not normal. I turned the pages of innumerable books of personal histories, trying to find the cornerstones that give the dramas and ecstasies of these personal histories meaning and sense.

I eventually found that cornerstone in the Miracle, in the awakening of the Consciousness, which demonstrated the futility of these personal histories and at the same time it showed the treasure to be found in them.

The personal histories are futile from the aspect of the awakening because we identify with our mind and we allow its unconscious functions to control our life and steer the boat of our life in one, and some time later just the opposite direction, depending on the actual desire or ambition dominating our mind. That is how page after page is filled in the history of our life until the last page arrives, and we realize the futility of all that happened before.

Our personal history may, however, have a very profound meaning if we become more wakeful and alert to these mind games, and recognize the Miracle, the wide open spaces of the Consciousness that is beyond our personal history. That pure consciousness was what I experienced as a child, and that is what I found again as a result of my regular meditation exercises that I had started a few years ago.

We must therefore wake up from our identification with our personal history, so as to be able to find our identity in the Miracle, the mystery of the Consciousness, instead of the world of the forms and shapes.

http://the-awakening-of-
consciousness.blogspot.com
Contact me at margif61@gmail.com

Published Books on Amazon.com

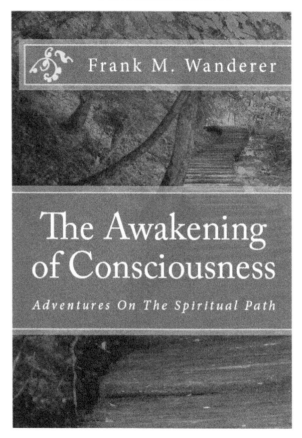

FRANK M. WANDERER: THE AWAKENING OF CONSCIOUSNESS

Paperback: 122 pages
Publisher: CreateSpace Independent Publishing Platform (January 14, 2014)
Language: English
ISBN-10: 1495200558
ISBN-13: 978-1495200557
Product Dimensions: 6 x 0.3 x 9 inches

We are all on a spiritual journey. This journey starts with birth and ends with death. Our life is a link between our date of birth and date of death. A link that contains all the secrets, dramas, tragedies and comedies of our lives, and we are so deeply involved in this performance that we tend to forget who we really are: the shining Consciousness. This book is about this spiritual journey.

Search on amazon for it or visit
http://fmw.kery.org

ERVIN K. KERY & FRANK M. WANDERER:

THE MIRACLE OF CONSCIOUSNESS

Paperback: 158 pages
Publisher: CreateSpace Independent Publishing Platform; 1 edition (June 4, 2014)
Language: English
ISBN-10: 1499115458
ISBN-13: 978-1499115451
Product Dimensions: 5 x 0.4 x 8 inches

There is a mysterious human dimension, the recognition of which shatters all our ideas about who we are, where we come from and what our mission in this world is. This is the realm of Consciousness: the final scientific and spiritual mystery. This book is about the mysteries and miracles of Consciousness. About the living spirit in action which, dressed up in the machinery of your body, discovers itself and the wonders of the world.

Search on amazon for it or visit
http://fmw.kery.org

FRANK M. WANDERER: THE FLAMES OF ALERTNESS

Paperback: 68 pages
Publisher: CreateSpace Independent Publishing Platform; 1 edition (October 8, 2014)
Language: English
ISBN-10: 1502748339
ISBN-13: 978-1502748331
Product Dimensions: 5 x 0.2 x 8 inches

This book will only reach you if a tiny flame of Alertness is burning in you. This awakening, small flame will be fanned up into a huge, blazing torch in you, and that torch will devour the accustomed, isolated world around you and place you back into the Oneness, which is your natural state of existence.

Search on amazon for it or visit
http://fmw.kery.org

FOR MORE BOOKS AND EBOOKS
AUTHORED BY FRANK M. WANDERER

PLEASE VISIT http://FMW.KERY.ORG

Made in United States
North Haven, CT
31 March 2022

17712903R00055